The Magical Christmas Tree

The Magical Christmas Tree

Written and Illustrated by
L.M. HAYNES

ELK PRESS

The Magical Christmas Tree
Copyright © 2020 by L.M. Haynes

Published in the United States of America
ISBN Paperback: 978-1-989942-09-3
ISBN Hardback: 978-1-989942-10-9
ISBN eBook: 978-1-929942-11-6

All rights reserved. No part of this publication may be reproduced, stored in a retrieval system or transmitted in any way by any means, electronic, mechanical, photocopy, recording or otherwise without the prior permission of the author except as provided by USA copyright law.

The opinions expressed by the author are not necessarily those of ELK Press.

Book design copyright © 2020. All rights reserved.
Written and Illustrated by L.M. Haynes

TO MY LOVING WIFE, AMY,
AND MY PRECIOUS DAUGHTERS,
CATIE, TINA, BERNADETTE, AND GINA.

IN LOVING MEMORY OF MY DAD, ROBERT HAYNES,
WHOSE LOVE OF CHRISTMAS IS INSTILLED IN
MY HEART.

The Scott's Christmas Tree Farm had been in their family for three generations. Every Christmas they would supply the local towns of New England with the most beautiful Christmas trees imaginable.

One Christmas many years ago, Grandpa Everett Scott would deliver a Christmas tree to a local family whose little girl had become very ill. This is the story of how that magical Christmas tree changed all their lives forever.

Everett Scott moved to Castle Falls as a young man with his beautiful wife Cecilia. They wanted to settle in a small New England town where they could own a home, raise a family, and be part of a close-knit community.

Everett supported his family for many years as the town handyman, carpenter, and gardener. However, his love for Christmas, which was instilled in him as a young boy, would forever keep his dream of owning a Christmas Tree Farm alive.

Castle Falls was a small town nestled in the hills of Vermont. It was a quaint New England town with beautiful old cape and colonial homes, winding mountain roads, and a main street lined with shops, restaurants, and markets.

Everett and Cecilia loved the life they had made in Castle Falls. As the years passed and their family grew, the Scotts became beloved in their community.

However, Grandpa Everett, as he became known in Castle Falls, did not let go of his dream of owning a Christmas Tree Farm. In 1959, that dream came true.

When Grandpa Everett purchased the land for the Family Tree Farm in 1959, it was nothing more that acres of open green field on the easterly edge of town.

That year, he planted row upon row of tiny evergreen trees on the land that would become known as Scott's Christmas Tree Farm.

It would take many years before the trees would be ready for sale, but Grandpa Everett was willing to take care of each and every tree until they would be ready to be brought to the market.

Steven

Andrew

Grandpa Everett continued his work around Castle Falls as the tiny trees on his farm began to grow. As the trees grow with each passing year, Everett would feed, cultivate, and trim each tree to a perfect shape.

His sons, Steven and Andrew, helped Everett work the farm as young boys. When they grew into fine young men, they married, started families of their own, and became his partners.

As the years passed, the tree farm required more and more of Everett's time. He and his sons would spend hours each week trimming and pruning each branch so that every single tree would have a perfect shape.

However, Everett noticed something different about one of his trees. While the other trees on his farm required much care, there was one special tree that did not. From the moment it was planted, this special tree grew perfectly each year. As it grew, it kept its cone-like shape, required no pruning, and seemed to develop a bright yellow glow. It seemed magical.

Now, in the heart of Castle Falls sat a beautiful brown framed home that belonged to the Anderson family. Little Ellie Anderson lived there with her mom, dad, and older brother Aaron.

It hadn't snowed very much the year Ellie got sick and Christmas was only a couple of weeks away. The people of Castle Falls always counted on there being a white Christmas, but this year, the entire town was still a blanket of green.

That same year, Ellie had begun not feeling well right after Thanksgiving. For days, she was running a fever, feeling very tired, and just wanted to sleep.

The doctors that Ellie visited with her mom and dad, Alison and Ed, were baffled by Ellie's illness. She had some type of virus that was making her very sick and the doctors were concerned. None of the medicine that they had given her seemed to work. With each passing day, Ellie's illness became worse.

Ellie's mom and dad both grew up in Castle Falls. They were High School sweethearts, then separated when they both went off to college.

Ed and Alison rekindled their romance when their college years ended and they returned home. They were married the following year, settled in Castle Falls, and started their family.

Alison worked as a nurse at a local doctor's office and Ed began his career working for a nearby land surveyor. They had both been raised with a strong Christian faith, but it was Alison's faith that had continued to grow over time.

With one week now remaining before Christmas, and Ellie still not feeling better, Aaron decided to write a letter to the local newspaper, the "Castle Falls Gazette". In his letter, he told the people of Castle Falls about Ellie's illness and asked for their prayers and support.

"Please keep my dear sister and my mom and dad in your thoughts and prayers", he wrote. "Nothing would be better than for the four of us to wake up on Christmas morning and have Ellie well again. Please help!"

—Aaron Anderson

Having seen Aaron's letter printed in the "Gazette", Alison could not help but be filled with pride." My thoughtful and caring son has asked for prayers for his sister, so it is prayers that she shall receive", she quietly thought to herself.

Relying on her faith, Alison stepped into the field behind her home and prayed. She quietly asked for the Lord's blessing upon her family and for his healing hand upon Ellie. "Dear, Lord," she asked. "Please bring us all a blessed Christmas and lay your healing hand upon my precious child, Ellie."

When Alison returned to the house after her time alone in prayer, she went over to the living room sofa and sat down by Ellie.

"How are you feeling today, my little Ellie?" Alison asked. "Not well, mommy," she replied. "But I have a good feeling that this will be a very special Christmas."

"So do I, dear. Is there a special gift that you have asked Santa for this year?"

"I would love for a little puppy to become part of our family. It really is the only gift that I have asked for," Ellie explained. "And I would also like to be well again."

It was now two days before Christmas. The weather forecast called for a snow storm on Christmas Eve. The good people of Castle Falls would be blessed with a white Christmas after all.

As Grandpa Everett sat in his barn that morning and read his newspaper, he came across the letter that had been written by Ellie's brother Aaron. "I want to do something to help this little girl and her family," Everett thought to himself. "But what?"

Christmas Eve had arrived. As he stared out the window of his home watching the Christmas snow fall, Grandpa Everett recalled what he had read in the newspaper two days earlier. Now, he knew exactly what he should do with his magical Christmas tree.

He called out to both Steven and Andrew who were working in the farm. "Boys, hurry and go cut down our magical tree. There is a family in need whose house is in the center of the town. Bring the tree to the Anderson home right now."

Steven and Andrew cut down the magical Christmas tree with great care, gently placed it in the back of the family pickup truck, and hurried to the home of the Anderson family.

Ed and Alison were so grateful when Steven and Andrew Scott delivered this magical Christmas tree to their home. When they saw the warm glow that came from the Scott's tree, they quickly removed the tree that they had set up and replaced it with this wondrous gift.

This magical Christmas tree instantly filled the Anderson's home with light, love, and hope for Ellie's healing.

When Steven and Andrew returned home and told their dad what had happened, Everett knew, that after all these years, his magical Christmas tree had found a home.

On this special Christmas Eve, Ellie Anderson could not sleep. Ever since the arrival of the magical Christmas tree earlier that day, she began feeling better. She knew in her heart that she was now going to get well.

She folded up the blanket that had been keeping her warm all these weeks and sat down beside the Christmas tree.

When she finally did become tired, Ellie happily walked to her bedroom, crawled into her bed, and off to sleep she went. Soon it would be Christmas morning.

When Ellie woke up on Christmas morning, she jumped out of bed, raced to the living room, and found a dark brown puppy curled up in a box under the Christmas tree.

Not only had her Christmas wish to get well come true, but Santa had delivered the most beautiful staffy bull terrier in the world.

His dark brindle coat and dark brown eyes brought a huge smile to her face. They fell in love with one another as soon as their eyes met.

Ellie would remember this Christmas always. On this magical Christmas, her mom's faith and prayers helped restore her health and gave her the gift of life.

But she also received the gift of a very adorable staffy bull terrier that she named Jem. By her mom's faith, the Grace of God, and the light from the magical Christmas tree, Ellie and Jem would share many more Christmas days together.

Then Jesus said to her, "Woman, you have great faith! Your request is granted." And her daughter was healed at that moment.

—Matthew 15:28 NIV

BOOK SUMMARY
"The Magical Christmas Tree"

It is Christmas time in the tiny town of Castle Falls. Little Ellie Anderson has been very ill and her Christmas wish this year is for healing and a new puppy. Grandpa Everett Scott is about to deliver a wondrous gift to the Anderson Family. Before this Christmas is over, the Scott and Anderson families will share the healing power of faith and a magical Christmas tree.

CPSIA information can be obtained
at www.ICGtesting.com
Printed in the USA
LVHW072055151120
671761LV00005B/17